WHO WAS THAT DOG I SAW YOU WITH, CHARLIE BROWN?

By Charles M. Schulz

Selected Cartoons from
You're You, Charlie Brown, Vol. 1

A FAWCETT CREST BOOK

FAWCETT PUBLICATIONS, INC., *Greenwich, Conn.*

Other Peanuts Books in Fawcett Crest Editions
Include the Following:

WHAT NOW, CHARLIE BROWN?   D1699
  (selected cartoons from The Unsinkable
  Charlie Brown, Vol. 1)

YOU'RE SOMEBODY SPECIAL, SNOOPY   D1722
  (selected cartoons from The Unsinkable
  Charlie Brown, Vol. 2)

YOU'VE GOT A FRIEND, CHARLIE BROWN D1754
  (selected cartoons from You'll Flip,
  Charlie Brown, Vol. 1)

TAKE IT EASY, CHARLIE BROWN   D1784
  (selected cartoons from You'll Flip,
  Charlie Brown, Vol. 2)

Only 50¢ Each—Wherever Paperbacks Are Sold

If your bookdealer is sold out, send cover price plus 15¢
each for postage and handling to Mail Order Department,
Fawcett Publications, Inc., Greenwich, Connecticut 06830.
Please order by number and title. Catalog available on
request.

WHO WAS THAT DOG I SAW YOU WITH, CHARLIE BROWN?

This book, prepared especially for Fawcett Publications, Inc.,
comprises the first half of YOU'RE YOU, CHARLIE BROWN,
and is reprinted by arrangement with Holt, Rinehart & Winston, Inc.

Copyright © 1967, 1968 by United Feature Syndicate, Inc.

All rights reserved, including the right to reproduce this book or
portions thereof in any form.

Printed in the United States of America
May 1973

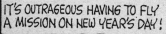

→

THAT'S HIS "HA-HA, YOU HAVE TO SHOVEL IT, AND I DON'T" DANCE!

NICE GOING...IT TOOK THAT STONE FOUR THOUSAND YEARS TO GET TO SHORE, AND NOW YOU'VE THROWN IT BACK!

EVERYTHING I DO MAKES ME FEEL GUILTY..

MY DAD LIKES TO HAVE ME COME DOWN TO THE BARBER SHOP, AND WAIT FOR HIM

NO MATTER HOW BUSY HE IS, EVEN IF THE SHOP IS FULL OF CUSTOMERS, HE ALWAYS STOPS TO SAY, "HI" TO ME...

I SIT HERE ON THE BENCH UNTIL SIX O'CLOCK, WHEN HE'S THROUGH, AND THEN WE RIDE HOME TOGETHER..

IT REALLY DOESN'T TAKE MUCH TO MAKE A DAD HAPPY...

THIS KID AT SCHOOL INSULTED ME, SEE?

NOW, WHAT I WANT YOU TO DO IS BITE HIM ON THE LEG TO HELP ME GET EVEN WITH HIM..

BITE SOMEONE....JUST TO GET EVEN?

HOW GAUCHE!

YOU CUT THAT OUT, YOU STUPID DOG!

WHY DON'T YOU GO SOME PLACE ELSE, AND SKATE?

→

PEOPLE WHO TALK TOO MUCH DESERVE TO BE INSULTED! THEY DESERVE TO HAVE OTHER PEOPLE WALK AWAY FROM THEM! TALKING TOO MUCH IS AN UNFORGIVABLE SOCIAL SIN! ABSOLUTELY UNFORGIVABLE!

THE DOCTOR

THE ONLY WAY TO DEAL WITH PEOPLE WHO TALK TOO MUCH IS TO LET THEM KNOW JUST HOW BORING THEY REALLY ARE...

THE DOCTOR

YOU CAN'T WASTE YOUR TIME WITH THEM... NO, SIR!

WHY SHOULD YOU SIT AND WASTE YOUR VALUABLE TIME WHILE SOME BORE TALKS ON AND ON ABOUT NOTHING?

THE DOCTOR

LIFE IS TOO SHORT TO WASTE IT LISTENING TO SOME PERSON WHO DOESN'T KNOW WHEN TO SHUT UP! TIME IS TOO VALUABLE! TIME IS...

SIGH!

SCHULZ

HI, GIRLS! WHERE..

GET OUT OF THE WAY!!!

WE'RE ON OUR WAY TO A "CRAB-IN"!

KER-CHUNK!

THANK YOU VERY MUCH, SNOOPY..

I WAS ALL OUT OF STAMPS

YOU'RE WELCOME

I'M THE ONLY ONE IN THE NEIGHBORHOOD WITH A POSTAGE METER

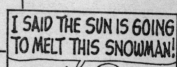

AND I GOT A VALENTINE FROM JOYCE AND I GOT ONE FROM PEGGY

AND I GOT ONE FROM ZELMA, AND JANELL, AND BOOTS, AND PAT, AND SYDNEY, AND WINNIE, AND JEAN, AND ROSEMARY, AND COURTNEY, AND FERN, AND MEREDITH ...

AND AMY, AND JILL, AND BETTY, AND MARGE, AND KAY, AND FRIEDA, AND ANNABELLE, AND SUE, AND EVA, AND JUDY, AND RUTH ...

AND BARBARA, AND OL'HELEN, AND ANN, AND JANE, AND DOROTHY, AND MARGARET, AND...

I CAN'T STAND IT... I JUST CAN'T STAND IT...

HOW IN THE WORLD DO YOU FIND
A SNOW-COVERED SUPPER DISH?!

AND I GOT A VALENTINE FROM CLARA, AND I GOT ONE FROM VIRGINIA AND ONE FROM RUBY..

AND I GOT ONE FROM JOY, AND CÉCILE, AND JULIE, AND HEDY, AND JUNE, AND MARIE...

AND KATHLEEN, AND MAGGIE, AND DIANE, AND VIVIAN, AND CHARLOTTE, AND TEKLA, AND LILLIAN, AND...

GOOD GRIEF!

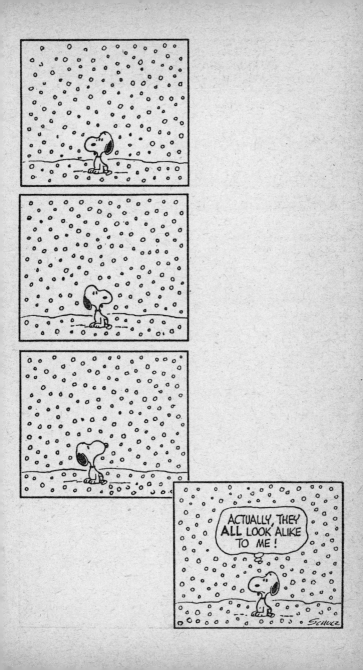

OKAY, I'M READY... THROW ME THE HOCKEY BALL!

YOU INVITED HER.. I DIDN'T

POOF!

PICK A CARD... ANY CARD..

I'M DEPRESSED, LINUS...

I NEED AN ENCOURAGING WORD TO CHEER ME UP

HAPPINESS LIES IN OUR DESTINY LIKE A CLOUDLESS SKY BEFORE THE STORMS OF TOMORROW DESTROY THE DREAMS OF YESTERDAY AND LAST WEEK!

I THINK THAT BLANKET IS DOING SOMETHING TO YOU!

THE EASTER BUNNY IS OUT IN OUR FRONT YARD!

SURE, HE IS..

HE'S HIDING EGGS...HE'S DOING A SPRING DANCE, AND HE'S HIDING EGGS ALL OVER THE FRONT LAWN...

UH HUH... SURE, HE IS...

I THINK I'LL GO OUT AND GATHER UP ALL THE EGGS

WHY DON'T YOU JUST DO THAT...

YOU MISS A LOT WHEN YOU SIT AND WATCH TV ALL DAY LONG...

I'VE DECIDED SOMETHING..

I'VE DECIDED TO BECOME A NURSE WHEN I GROW UP!

HOW DID YOU HAPPEN TO DECIDE THAT?

I LIKE WHITE SHOES

I CAN'T TALK TO THAT LITTLE RED-HAIRED GIRL BECAUSE SHE'S SOMETHING AND I'M NOTHING

IF I WERE SOMETHING AND SHE WERE NOTHING, I COULD TALK TO HER, OR IF SHE WERE SOMETHING AND I WERE SOMETHING, THEN I COULD TALK TO HER...

OR IF SHE WERE NOTHING AND I WERE NOTHING, THEN I ALSO COULD TALK TO HER...BUT SHE'S SOMETHING AND I'M NOTHING SO I CAN'T TALK TO HER...

FOR A NOTHING, CHARLIE BROWN, YOU'RE REALLY SOMETHING!

I WONDER IF I WOULDN'T BE MORE POPULAR IF I HAD A NEW NAME...

THE WRONG NAME CAN BE A REAL HINDRANCE TO A PERSON'S FUNCTIONING IN SOCIETY.. I THINK A NAME WHICH IS CONSISTENT WITH A PERSON'S PERSONALITY IS IMPORTANT

I WONDER WHAT WOULD BE A GOOD NAME FOR ME...

HOW ABOUT "SUPERMOUTH"?

I'VE GOT TO STOP THIS BUSINESS OF TALKING WITHOUT THINKING...

SCHULZ

IN A WAY, YOU'RE QUITE LUCKY, SCHROEDER...

IF YOU EVER GO INTO THE ARMY, THEY WON'T PUT YOU IN THE FRONT LINES...

YOU COULD PLAY THE PIANO FOR THE OFFICERS WHILE THEY EAT!

AAUGH!

IT'S THE SECOND DAY OF THE BIG MASTERS GOLF TOURNAMENT IN AUGUSTA, GEORGIA..

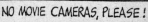

NO MOVIE CAMERAS, PLEASE!

HERE'S THE WORLD-FAMOUS GOLF PRO LINING UP HIS PUTT ON THE SIXTEENTH GREEN..........

DO YOU REALIZE THAT THEY MAY HAVE TO REPLANT EVERY TREE IN THIS PARK?

I CAN'T STAND IT.. I JUST CAN'T STAND IT...

HAPPY FATHER'S DAY *from your rare gem.*

HI, ROY... I SUPPOSE YOU'RE WONDERING WHAT I'M DOING...

I'VE JUST MADE MY DAD A HAND-MADE FATHER'S DAY CARD..

→

I HAVE A MESSAGE FOR YOU...

MOM SAY'S GET YOUR STUPID SELF IN THERE, AND CLEAN UP YOUR STUPID ROOM!

I'M SURE SHE DIDN'T SAY IT QUITE LIKE THAT

SO I ELABORATED A LITTLE..

IF SHE'D JUST MISS, MAYBE I'D HAVE AN OPENING TO SUGGEST THAT WE QUIT..WHY DOESN'T SHE EVER MISS? MISS! MISS! MISS! RATS! SHE NEVER MISSES! WHY DON'T I JUST TELL HER I'M GOING HOME?

THAT'S WHAT I THINK I'LL DO... I THINK I'LL JUST TELL HER THAT I HAVE TO QUIT AND GO HOME... I THINK I'LL JUST DROP THE ROPE, AND TELL HER I'M GOING HOME.... MISS! MISS! MISS!

MY ARM IS GETTING NUMB... I CAN'T EVEN FEEL MY FINGERS ANY MORE.. I THINK I'LL JUST THROW THE ROPE DOWN, AND TELL HER I'M QUITTING... I THINK I'LL JUST LET GO, AND WALK AWAY... I..

TEN THOUSAND! TEN THOUSAND AND ONE, TEN THOUSAND AND TWO..

SIGH!

THERE'S ANOTHER GOOD THING ABOUT PLAYING NIGHT GAMES, CHARLIE BROWN..

SAY YOU'RE PITCHING A LOUSY GAME, SEE, AND WE WANT TO GET YOU OUT OF THERE...WELL, ALL WE HAVE TO DO IS COME OUT TO THE MOUND AND BLOW OUT YOUR CANDLE!

POOF!

I THINK WE'D BETTER STICK TO DAY GAMES!

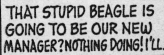

IT'S KIND OF NICE NOT BEING MANAGER..

ON THE NIGHT BEFORE OUR GAMES I ALWAYS USED TO LIE AWAKE WORRYING...

I WONDER IF OUR NEW MANAGER IS LYING AWAKE WORRYING...

"YOU'RE OUT!!"

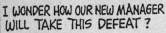

IF I HAVE A BIRTHDAY PARTY, WILL YOU GIRLS COME?

WELL, FRANKLY, CHARLIE BROWN, WE'D RATHER NOT...

BUT IF WE CAN'T FIND ANYTHING ELSE TO DO, AND IF THERE'S NOTHING GOOD ON TV THAT DAY, WE MIGHT CONSIDER COMING...

IT'S FUN TO GIVE A PARTY WHEN EVERYONE'S SO ENTHUSIASTIC

BEEP!

I HAVEN'T BEEPED YOU IN A LONG TIME

I HAVEN'T MISSED IT A BIT!

SCHULZ

POW!

YOU HAVE CUTE TOES, CHARLIE BROWN!

DON'T YOU EVER GET TIRED OF THAT BLANKET?

KLUNK!

YOU CAN'T DO ANYTHING, CAN YOU, CHARLIE BROWN?

WELL, SO LONG, ROY... I'M OFF TO CAMP!

THIS YEAR I'M IN CHARGE OF A TENT... I'M ALMOST LIKE A COUNSELOR...ISN'T THAT GREAT?

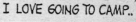

I LOVE GOING TO CAMP..

FOR A GIRL LIKE ME, IT'S THE NEXT BEST THING TO BEING IN THE INFANTRY!

SCHULZ

HELLO, GIRLS... I'M "PEPPERMINT" PATTY, YOUR TENT MONITOR...

ACTUALLY, MY NAME REALLY ISN'T "PEPPERMINT" PATTY...THAT'S JUST A NICK-NAME MY DAD GAVE ME... HE ALSO CALLS ME HIS "RARE GEM"

NOW, WHAT ARE YOUR NAMES?

AFTER ALL THAT, WHAT CAN WE SAY?

NOW Peanuts Jewelry

Each item is 14 Kt. gold finish, hand-crafted cloisonné in brilliant colors, exquisitely designed by Aviva. Items shown in actual size. Complete satisfaction guaranteed or money refunded.

No. 10 pin $3

No. 11 pin $3

No. 12 pin $3

No. 13A pierced $3
No. 13B non-pierced $3

No. 14 pin $3

No. 15 pin $3

No. 16 pin $3

No. 17A pierced $3
No. 17B non-pierced $3

No. 18 pin $3

No. 19 pin $3

No. 20 pin $3

© United Feature Syndicate, Inc. 1971

No. 21 pin $3

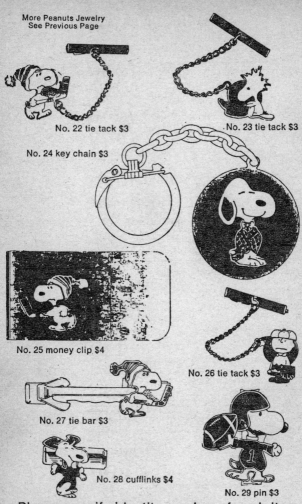

No. 22 tie tack $3

No. 23 tie tack $3

No. 24 key chain $3

No. 25 money clip $4

No. 26 tie tack $3

No. 27 tie bar $3

No. 28 cufflinks $4

No. 29 pin $3

Please specify identity number of each item ordered and add 25¢ for each item to cover postage and handling. Personal check or money order. No cash. Send orders to HAMILTON HOUSE, Cos Cob, Conn. 06807.

© United Feature Syndicate, Inc. 1971